Seasons

by Janet Allison Brown

Aladdin/Watts
London • Sydney

Contents

© Aladdin Books Ltd 2000

Designed and produced by
Aladdin Books Ltd
28 Percy Street
London W1T 2BZ

First published in
Great Britain in 2000 by
Franklin Watts
96 Leonard Street
London EC2A 4XD

ISBN 0 7496 4852 X

A catalogue record for this book is
available from the British Library.

Printed in the U.A.E.

All rights reserved

Editor
Jim Pipe

Literacy Consultant
Ann Hawken
Oxford Brookes University
Westminster Institute of Education

Design
Flick Book Design and Graphics

Picture Research
Brian Hunter Smart

Have you felt the hot sun in summer or icy winds in winter?

Have you seen blossom in spring or the falling leaves in autumn?

These are the seasons, the different times of the year.

Boats in summer

Each season brings changes. Days grow longer in spring, then grow shorter again in the autumn.

In summer the sun shines longest – it is a good time for a boat ride!

Every year, the weather changes from warm to hot to cool to cold.

The coldest days of the year are in winter. Rain turns to snow and people stay indoors.

Winter snow

6

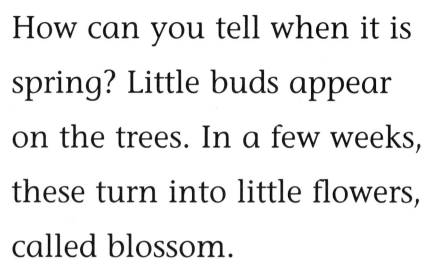

How can you tell when it is spring? Little buds appear on the trees. In a few weeks, these turn into little flowers, called blossom.

Apple
blossom

Spring

Spring is when things start to grow.

It is often cold and wet.

Spring rain

After a while the days grow
longer and the skies are brighter.
But the rain keeps falling!

Spring can be a time for **Umbrellas**
umbrellas and splashing in puddles!

In spring, farmers plough their fields and plant seeds in the ground. The spring rains fall on the seeds and help them to grow.

Ploughing

Seeds grow

Many baby animals are born now.

Birds build nests and lay their eggs.

In a few weeks the eggs hatch

into chicks!

Chicks

12

Summer is full of bright colours. The trees are heavy with leaves and some fields are a blanket of flowers.

Summer flowers

Little apples

At the beach

Summer is the season for being outdoors. The days are long and bright.

The hot, sunny weather is perfect for walks in the country or days at the beach.

In the country

15

In summer, the grass
grows tall and thick.
Butterflies flutter from
flower to flower.

Bee

Butterfly

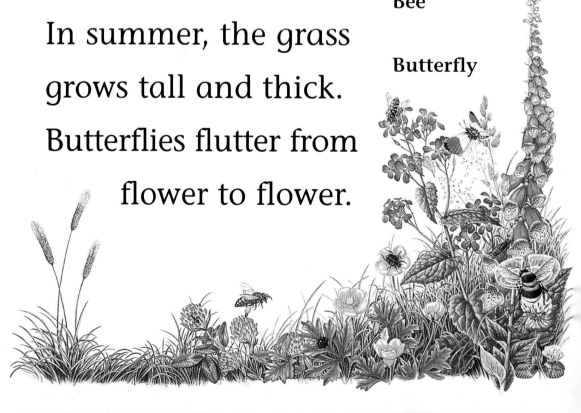

Rabbit

Bees buzz through the air. They are busy using flowers to make honey!

You will often see rabbits nibble on grass. Be quiet or their long ears will hear you coming!

18

In autumn, the weather becomes cooler and the days grow shorter.

The leaves change from green to gold and red. They fall from the trees and blow about in the autumn wind.

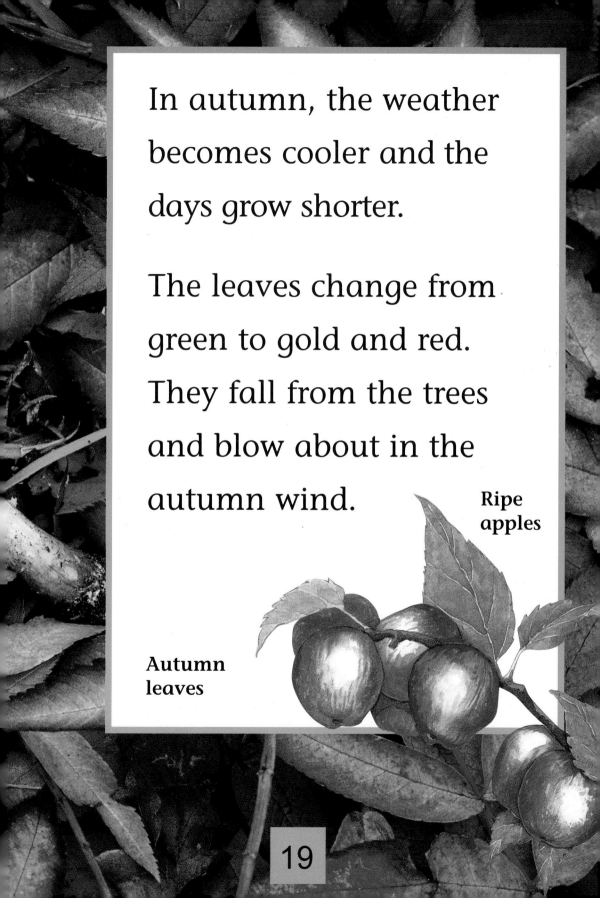

Ripe apples

Autumn leaves

Collecting grapes

In autumn, farmers are busy picking fruit and other crops.

This farmer grows grapes. When they are dry, they will be called raisins. Do you like eating raisins?

Squirrel

Animals know that in autumn cold weather is on its way.

Squirrels gather nuts to eat in winter. Birds feed on berries, and some fly away to warmer places.

Blackbird eating berries

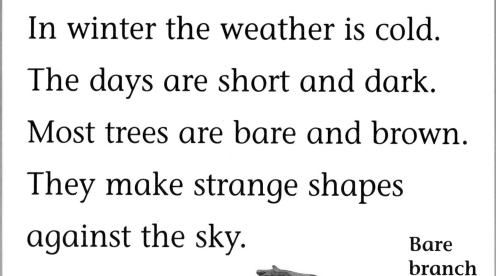

In winter the weather is cold.

The days are short and dark.

Most trees are bare and brown.

They make strange shapes
against the sky.

Bare
branch

Winter trees

When it gets really cold, snow falls and the world turns white. Drops of water become icicles.

Icicles

Hare

This mouse sleeps through winter. Some hares grow a white coat to hide in the snow.

Mouse

Under the snow, nothing grows – everything waits for spring!

25

In some places the seasons are all alike. Rainforests are always hot, but some seasons are more rainy.

Rainforest

South Pole

When it does
not rain, deserts
have no seasons.

Desert

The South Pole has two seasons.
The sun shines almost all the time in
summer, and almost never in winter.

27

Can You Find?

Can you work out what season it is by looking at animals or plants? Look at these pictures and see!

Blossom

Butterfly

Hare

Ripe apples

Chick

Mushroom

Icicles

Answers on
page 32.

Clue: Look at pages 7, 11,
16, 18, 19, 24 and 25.

Do You Know?

Look at these four pictures of the same tree. Do you know which one shows it in spring, summer, autumn or winter?

2

1

The answers
are on
page 32.

3

4

Index

ANSWERS TO QUESTIONS

Page 28-29 – Blossom appears in **spring** • This hare has a white coat in **winter** • You see most butterflies in **summer** • Apples are ripe in **autumn** • Most chicks hatch from eggs in **spring** • Most mushrooms appear in **autumn** • Icicles appear on cold **winter** days.

Pages 30-31 – **1** shows the tree in spring • **2** shows the tree in winter • **3** shows the tree in summer • **4** shows the tree in autumn.

Photocredits: Abbreviations: t-top, m-middle, b-bottom, r-right, l-left., Cover 1, 3, 8, 12-13, 14, 15, 18-19, 24, 25, 27 both, 28bl, 29tr, 29br – Digital Stock. 4, 16, 20, 26 – Corbis Images. 5, 6-7, 9, 22-23, 28ml – Select Pictures. 10-11, 11r, 28mr, 29tl – Stockbyte. 21 – John Foxx Images. 28-29 all – Sylvestris Fotoservice/FLPA-Images of Nature.
Illustrators: Wayne Ford – for Wildlife Art Ltd; Elizabeth Sawyer.